STOKE
OLD AND NEW

RICHARD TALBOT

Published by E.P Publishing Limited 1977

This edition first published 1977 by
EP Publishing Limited,
East Ardsley, Wakefield, West Yorkshire
England

ISBN 0 7158 1190 8

Please address all enquiries to EP Publishing Limited
(address as above)

Printed and bound in Great Britain by
Fretwell & Brian Limited, Silsden, Keighley, Yorkshire.

Introduction

The City of Stoke-on-Trent consists of a string of towns called Tunstall, Burslem, Hanley, Stoke, Fenton and Longton. They all fit under the title of 'the Potteries', by which name the district is identified world-wide as the seat of the pottery industry. These six towns were linked together in 1910 to become Stoke-on-Trent and in 1925 City status was conferred.

To those who do not reside in the area, the word 'Potteries' conjures up an image of smoke-stained bottle ovens, slag heaps, thick smog and old pottery manufactories belonging to the early nineteenth century. They can hardly be blamed for this impression, for picture postcards of the district on sale until a few years ago encouraged this belief. But that was not the whole picture, and those who looked for it could find beauty within the boundaries of the city.

I could easily have compiled a book containing photographs of old bottle ovens, slag heaps and the like, for each city throughout the land must bear the scars of its own individual industrial past, but I have endeavoured to create a different image of the Potteries, to show a city which is full of its own character and charm.

Over the last twenty years, there can hardly be another city within the United Kingdom which has changed so completely and so rapidly as the city of Stoke on Trent. In travelling around the area with my photographer, Ronald Foster, I have been impressed with several factors. Firstly, it is remarkable just what changes have taken place with the assistance of environmental grants from central government. Many derelict sites have been reclaimed, and old buildings and churches have received a face-lift. Ambitious schemes have been undertaken which, only a few years ago, would have seemed impossible to carry out.

Secondly, and this is the more surprising, Stoke-on-Trent is a much greener place than it used to be. Where old derelict buildings once stood, there now lie beautifully-kept lawns with shrubs and trees. The City Council have taken full advantage of all the means available to carry out this work, and they should receive full credit.

In 1975 Stoke-on-Trent celebrated its Golden Jubilee as a City. This year (1977) the whole country and Commonwealth celebrate the Queen's Jubilee, and therefore it is perhaps appropriate that this book should be compiled and published at this time to celebrate two special occasions in the lives of the kind-hearted people of those towns, villages and hamlets known as the Potteries.

I must record special thanks to my photographer, Ronald Foster, who has reproduced many old photographs which at first sight were considered unsuitable because of their poor quality. He has also performed amazing feats on the top of ladders in order to retake some of the scenes, and his expert knowledge in the developing and printing of photographs is clearly seen within this book. I must also record my appreciation to Mr. A. Lawton and Mrs. Pointon for the loan of photographs and the assistance given to me by the staff of the City Reference Library. My thanks too to Gordon Boulton, who has so kindly drawn the sketch on plate 15.

The book commences at the northern end of the city, taking the reader through the towns of Tunstall, Burslem, Hanley and Stoke. From Stoke it goes to Hartshill and then down to Boothen, Hanford, Trentham and Longton, finishing up at Fenton.

I hope readers will agree that this book shows our city to a better advantage than ever before, demonstrating that it has, in fact, many views of character and interest if only we are prepared to look for them.

So this book is a record of a changing city, and as far as I know, it is the only one which shows both the Old and the New. I hope that it will appeal not only to the inhabitants of Stoke-on-Trent, but also to the thousands who visit the district each year, and those who are aware of the products of artistic beauty which are produced in its factories and appreciated all over the world.

Richard Talbot
Penkhull, Stoke-on-Trent,
1977.

Contents

Tunstall - 1893

Christ Church, Tunstall, which was built in 1831, was the first church erected in the town. It was built with stone from the neighbouring quarries of Chell at a cost of £4,000. This drawing shows it in a delightful rural setting.

Tunstall - 1976
The church still stands, though the low spire has been removed from the tower. The little country lane has now turned into a busy highway and that quaint setting of the past will remain forever just a picture.

Brownhills, Burslem - c. 1870

Brownhills Toll Gate, as it was known, gives a very good picture of the rural setting which existed just outside the towns of Burslem and Tunstall. This Toll Gate had two gates, one leading to Burslem and the other to the town of Newcastle which was just outside the city boundary.

Brownhills, Burslem - 1976
Brownhills today is just an extension of the pottery towns, and modern housing development has pushed the green fields farther away. Every trace of the past has gone except for the division of the roads.

Swan Square, Burslem - 1919
In the centre of the photograph stands the Central Methodist Church, built in 1801. This huge depressing structure, black with the smoke of over a hundred years, was recently demolished.

Swan Square, Burslem - 1976
Although Burslem now looks considerably brighter, this part of town has not changed very much. A new church to replace the old, a tree, a few plants, seats for shoppers—and the whole atmosphere is altered.

Queen Street, Burslem - 1903
This photograph shows the Wedgwood Institute, opened in 1869 as a memorial to Josiah Wedgwood. The building has a remarkable and elaborate front, mainly in the Venetian Gothic Style, and includes terra-cotta panels and other decorative features. The building at the top of the street on the right is the public indoor market, built in 1879.

Queen Street, Burslem - 1976
The Wedgwood Institute still stands dominating the street and rightly so, for since a recent face-lift it has become one of the focal points of the town. Many of the old shops have been replaced by new buildings, and the tower from the top of the market hall was removed many years ago. Just to the right of the street lamp can be seen the nameplate of Clayhanger Street, the name of which forms the title of one of Arnold Bennett's books.

Market Place, Burslem - c. 1900
Old Burslem as Arnold Bennett knew it. Here can be seen in the background the Italian styled old Town Hall, built of stone during the 1850s. In addition to its splendid entrance hall, which has a fine staircase, it is adorned with a golden angel, which stands precariously on a golden orb at the top of the tower. The tram lines here are laid for the steam trams; they had not yet been 'converted' to electricity, for no cable support poles are to be seen.

Market Place, Burslem - 1976

The money spent in revitalizing the mother town of the Potteries has not been wasted, for Burslem now presents a clean, smart and attractive face to the world without having lost its old-world charm and character. Partly out of view behind the old Town Hall can be seen the new one, built in 1911, and now used as a theatre.

Market Place, Burslem - c.1912
Almost the same view as No. 9, but on the right can be seen ladies milling round the open market stalls. The cable support poles towering over the old gas lamps show that electric tram cars have appeared in the intervening years.

Market Place, Burslem - 1976
Burslem old Town Hall replaced an earlier Town Hall built in 1760, which was demolished to make way for this building (described in no. 9). The outside has recently received a face-lift under the environmental grant scheme, while inside the building has been converted into a leisure centre. Notice how clean the air now is here and throughout the Potteries.

Century Street, Hanley - c.1874

This photograph shows evidence of hand-drawn alterations, but though it may be slightly exaggerated it gives an accurate impression of Hanley at this time.

Century Street, Hanley - 1976
Although Century Street itself remains unchanged, Hanley has practically been rebuilt over the past twenty years. Nearly all the bottle ovens have disappeared, and what has now become the main shopping centre of the Potteries is a much cleaner and healthier place in which to shop, work and live.

Town Road, Hanley - 1829

This sketch by Mr F. E. Watts appeared in the 'Weekly Sentinel' in 1829, and was based on drawings of one hundred years earlier. It shows Market Square, looking towards what is now Town Road, but was then a cul-de-sac with a collection of factories built around it. On the right is the old bank and on the left can be seen the Golden Lion and, higher up the road, the Sea Lion public house.

Town Road, Hanley - 1976
All that remains of the old is the Sea Lion public house, which stands out of view half way up Town Road. St. John's Church, built in 1788-90 at a cost of £6,000, can just be made out in the distance.

Parliament Row, Hanley - late 19th century
A solitary lamp dominates Parliament Row, which can be seen here with traders on a busy market day. The horse-drawn carts made ideal stands from which to sell produce. The young boys were probably waiting in the hope of earning a few pence by holding a horse while its master was away.

Parliament Row, Hanley - 1976
The buildings on the right have been replaced again and again over the intervening years. That solitary lamp would now be in the middle of a busy road and the horse and cart would stand little chance against modern-day traffic. See what an attractive town Hanley has become, with modern buildings, trees and shrubs.

Parliament Row, Hanley - 1897

This photograph was taken on the occasion of Queen Victoria's Diamond Jubilee, when the streets were decorated with flags and bunting. The crowds were waiting for the procession of brass bands and civic leaders to pass by.

Parliament Row, Hanley - 1976
This photograph is very new indeed. The bank with its attractive vertical lines, together with the new Woolworths store, form a striking contrast to the old scene. Nothing remains of the past except the name.

Parliament Row, Hanley - 1919

The Lyric Theatre, on the left of this photograph, opened in about 1912 and was one of the many silent picture houses existing in the Potteries at that time. It wasn't there for long, however; the Lyric closed its doors in the early 1920s. Note the admission charges—3d and 6d. Next door stands F. W. Woolworth & Co., also then known by the name of the 3d and 6d store.

Parliament Row, Hanley - 1976
New development in Hanley has changed this picture beyond any recognition with the past, except that Woolworth's still occupy the same site after nearly sixty years in the town.

Market Square, Hanley - 1903

If this view looks familiar, it is because market gardeners and local traders bring their produce and goods here to sell on market day just as they did in 1903, and had been doing for over a century before that. The large building to the left of the photograph is the indoor market, built in 1849, which today is still used for its original purpose.

Market Square, Hanley - 1976
This photograph was not taken on market day, thus allowing us a clear view of what the Square looks like today. The view seems much greener, because of the flourishing trees, though most of the original buildings still remain. The old market hall can still be seen to the left of the picture, and the old buildings on the right have only undergone a slight modernisation of the shop fronts. The only major change is that the Angel Hotel and the Grapes Hotel, which stood at the top of the Square, were both demolished in the mid-1960s and have been replaced by new shops.

Fountain Square, Hanley - 1919
Central in this photograph stands a bronze statue of a Greek maiden, presented to the town of Hanley in 1859 by William Brownfield to mark his year as Mayor. During the 1920s it was removed to Northwood Park to enable road development to take place.

Fountain Square, Hanley - 1976
The greener, brighter look of Stoke-on-Trent is self-evident in this photograph. The statue, cleaned and fitted with a new arm, made a triumphant return to the new-look Fountain Square in 1974, and has been re-sited amid the fountains, gardens and seats for shoppers. This pair of photographs shows just how much more casual ladies' clothing has become over the years. Compare the young girls in the centre of the old picture with the little girl playing in the fountain to the left of the new photograph.

Fountain Square, Hanley - c.1910
This severely classical building is Hanley's old Town Hall, built in the early nineteenth century. During the 1840s it was the centre of the Chartist Riots, and at one time cannons, relics of those days, stood outside. The hall was once occupied by a battalion of soldiers from Chester, and it is known that the Riot Act was read out from the steps of the building to the raging mob gathered outside.

Fountain Square, Hanley - 1976
The old Town Hall was purchased by Lloyds Bank in 1886 when the town council moved its civic offices to another building in the town. In 1935-6 the present building seen in this photograph was erected in its place.

Crown Bank, Hanley - 1900
In the exact centre of this picture, only half showing, is the old Town Hall. Note how the people of that time could stroll about the town with ease, with no fear of being run down by passing traffic.

Crown Bank, Hanley - 1976
Demolish the old, preserve the best! This photograph shows that the old buildings on the left of the previous view have been replaced by spacious modern shops, while those on the right have been preserved, keeping their original character. Central is the new bank, built in 1936, which replaced the old Town Hall.

Lamb Street, Hanley - 1897
This photograph was taken on a market day - the stalls can be seen in the market square in the distance. The fine building on the left had been standing for ten years.

Lamb Street, Hanley - 1976

The row of large shops on the left now belongs to just one company, and the new canopy covering the footpath was completed in 1961. Although the modern shop fronts are not in keeping with the original architecture of the building, they and the new shops on the right give an impression of space and cleanliness typical of the streamlined seventies.

Lamb Street, Hanley - 1948

This view was taken from the opposite end of the road from nos. 31 and 32. A very busy street on a market day, but Lamb Street was quiet on the day this photograph was taken except for the motor cars which even in those early days were lined up the kerbside. Barclays Bank in the foreground was built in 1891 as the Birmingham Penny Bank.

Lamb Street, Hanley - 1976
In 1961 Barclays Bank was taken over by the large department store which now extends halfway down the street. The clean new buildings on the left are an interesting contrast to the old, blackened buildings remaining on the right. Nowadays Lamb Street is almost traffic-free.

Trinity Street, Hanley - c.1925
This photograph of the Empire Picture House was taken from the Trinity Street entrance, the other entrance being situated in Piccadilly.

Trinity Street, Hanley - 1976
A most unattractive sample of modern architecture. This shopping arcade has replaced the Empire, which was closed in about 1960.

Trinity Street, Hanley - turn of the century

Known as the Grand Theatre of Varieties, this theatre was built at a cost of £25,000 and opened in 1898. It was described in 1920 as the handsomest and most commodious house of entertainment in the northern part of the county, and indeed in the whole district between Birmingham and Manchester. It was situated opposite the Empire Picture House, shown in plate 35.

37

Trinity Street, Hanley - 1975
The innovation of the flickering shadows on a bioscope screen spelled doom for the Grand – at first a five-minute feature was provided in the variety programme, but by 1931 films had conquered the Grand and it became a cinema. A year later, on May 11th, It was burnt down, and was replaced by a modern purpose-built cinema called the Odeon. However, declining audiences caused the Odeon to close in 1975 and at the time of writing a decision on the future of the building is still awaited.

Pall Mall, Hanley - 1919

Just a quiet street, looking down to Marsh Street and the Y.M.C.A. On the right, just before the bottom of the road, stands the Theatre Royal, opened in 1871 and later enlarged twice before it was burnt down in 1949 and rebuilt in 1950-51.

Pall Mall, Hanley - 1976
The old buildings are dwarfed by the new 'post office tower' of Hanley, which has replaced the old Y.M.C.A. Most of the other buildings remain, though their frontages have been altered. Most cities have seen the transformation of theatres to bingo halls, and the Theatre Royal is regrettably no exception.

Howard Place, Shelton - 1910
Quiet and serene, the district known as Shelton was just a stopping place between Stoke and Hanley; many businessmen lived there in the high-class residences. A double track section of tram line can be seen here, for the road is wide enough to take two lines and so avoid the use of passing loops and track mergers.

Howard Place, Shelton - 1976

The tram stop has been replaced by traffic lights, and extensive road widening has taken place to accommodate the ever-increasing rush hour traffic. Shelton is no longer just a stopping place – it has become an extension of Stoke and Hanley. The buildings to the left and right of the photograph have remained unchanged over the years, the only addition being the building in the background, erected in 1958 as the Mellor Green Laboratories of the British Ceramic Research Association, but used today as an office block by a national company.

Liverpool Road, Stoke - 1911

This road was first known by the name 'New Road', for it was not cut until about 1820 and was in fact the new road from Stoke to Hanley. Notice the words 'wait here for cars' which appear on the cable supports for the electric trams.

Liverpool Road, Stoke - 1976
Liverpool Road looks much the same as it did in 1911, though the surface of the road has changed and a coat of paint has brightened up the appearance of the shops. The main change is on the right of the photograph, where the Co-op Bank and a dance hall above have appeared.

Liverpool Road junction with Church Street, Stoke - 1908
The old Queens Hotel, demolished in 1968-9, forms the centre of this picture and was at one time a popular meeting place for the unemployed men during the years of the Depression. As you can see, all the people are looking towards the camera, for such an instrument was seldom seen in the early part of this century in the working-class towns of the Potteries.

Liverpool Road junction with Church Street, Stoke - 1976
The Queens Hotel has been replaced by a small garden and trees. A one-way traffic system operates through the town to speed up the traffic flow, and there has been extensive road widening, for the building on the left has had the ground floor frontage set back to make way for the new pavement.

Church Street, Stoke - 1909
The stark factory building on the left of this picture belonged to Spode Limited and was demolished in 1929 to make way for a neat row of shops. Note the large display of straw boaters outside the shop just to the right of the photograph.

Church Street, Stoke - 1976
Many of the old buildings have changed over the years and others have been replaced. One which does remain is the large black and white building on the right, which dates from about 1790 and has been partly used as a chemist's shop since the early nineteenth century. The lines of traffic and proliferation of signs and notices of all sorts give this busy road junction an atmosphere quite different from the more leisured view opposite.

Campbell Place, Stoke - 1908
The statue of Colin Minton Campbell stood serene in the centre of Stoke from 1887 to the end of the 1930s. He was thrice Mayor of Stoke, and the grandson of Thomas Minton the famous potter. On the left stands the Grapes public house, a substantial late eighteenth century building. Although somewhat altered, perhaps at the time of its conversion to an Inn in about 1865, it retained a Georgian facade until its demolition in 1960, and was probably the oldest building in the town.

Campbell Place, Stoke - 1976
Stoke town is now hardly recognisable. Campbell's statue has been removed to a suitable site outside the Minton China works about two hundred yards away, and new shops and a busy one-way traffic system have replaced the old-world charm. The decorative iron railings in the old photograph protected the monument from the pedestrians; the new mass-produced railings shown here protect the pedestrians from the traffic.

Campbell Place, Stoke, looking south - 1915
These buildings were erected just after the turn of the century, and replaced a pottery works which stood on the site for many years. Under the pavement ran the Newcastle canal which linked up with the Trent and Mersey canal a few hundred yards away, near to Stoke Railway Station. To the right of the picture is the old Majestic Cinema—see plate 53. Campbell Place was previously called Eldon Place.

Campbell Place, Stoke, looking south - 1976
The old shops remain though their frontages have been changed many times over the years. The old cinema where I spent many happy hours of my childhood has now gone, and has been replaced by yet another branch of a well-known store.

Campbell Place, Stoke, looking north - 1919
To the right of the picture is the old Majestic Cinema, built in 1913 and demolished in 1957 after a short life. Central in the photograph is the Wheat Sheaf Hotel, from which, in 1818, stage coaches ran to Liverpool and London. Just in front of the hotel stands the statue of Colin Minton Campbell.

Campbell Place, Stoke, looking north - 1976
Very little of old Stoke remains; new stores, offices and pubs have replaced all the old buildings. Nearly the only remaining landmark is the chimney in the background of the famous Spode pottery works, now identified by that name.

London Road, Stoke - 1919

The long three-storey building on the right is the pottery works of Minton China and dates from about the middle of the nineteenth century. The first building on the left, with the unusual port-hole style windows, is Stoke Library, designed by Charles Lynam and built in 1877 at a cost of £2,850. It was formally opened by Mr. Colin Minton Campbell on 8 November 1878. The second building is the old Minton Institute which was built as a school of art in 1858-9 and is now the City Health Department.

London Road, Stoke - 1976
Here can be seen a fine example of architecture which has been hidden away for many years beneath industrial smoke and dirt. A clean-down in 1974 has revealed these buildings as being highly distinctive. Minton's old 'pot works' has now been replaced by attractive gardens and a new factory has been built, set back a few yards from the road. The decorative lamps from outside the library have also disappeared, but one distinctive feature still remains after years of faithful service, with nothing in return except perhaps a new coat of red paint—the old pillar box.

Church Street, Stoke - 1919
The road was raised at this point and known as the bridge; the barges loaded with coal and clay passed under the road through the tunnel of the Newcastle canal.

Church Street, Stoke - 1976
The canal through Stoke ceased to be used in the early 1930s, but the tunnel still remains, having been bricked up at either end. Over the years, there have been few architectural changes in this street though the shops have been brightened up.

Church Street, Stoke - 1906

To the left of this photograph stands the old Music Hall first known as The Eagle and then later as the Queen's Palace. On the right is Boots Cash Chemists, as it was then called. Nearly all the buildings in this street were erected in the mid or late nineteenth century.

Church Street, Stoke - 1976
Little development has taken place in Church Street over the last seventy years, though each building exhibits a new façade. The old music hall first gave way to the Rialto Dance Hall and is now used as the Stoke Conservative Club. Boots the Chemists closed in 1975, as part of a reorganisation plan. Note the change in the style of public transport from the old electric tram to the modern comfortable bus.

Glebe Street, Stoke - 1913
The drinking fountain built into the wall of Stoke Churchyard was a popular meeting place for children and adults alike. It remained until the 1930s, when the road was widened to accommodate the increase in traffic.

Glebe Street, Stoke - 1976
The trees have grown in sixty years and unfortunately obstruct the view of Stoke Parish Church, which has recently undergone a stone-cleaning operation. In the foreground, yet more road widening has taken place.

Church Street, Stoke - 1820

This picture was drawn only a few years before Stoke Old Church was demolished in 1826. It is likely that the nave was pre-Norman with the chancel added or rebuilt in the early fourteenth century. Beneath what was the entrance to this church lies the tomb of Josiah Wedgwood.

Church Street, Stoke - 1976
All that remains of Stoke Old Church are these arches, which were re-erected in 1881 by Charles Lynam on the very spot where they had stood fifty-five years before. Josiah Wedgwood's tomb is just below the central support, and nearby are those of Josiah Spode and Thomas Minton.

Glebe Street, Stoke - 1901
On the left can be seen Stoke Town Hall, the largest and most imposing of the six within the city. The building was started in 1834 but not completed until 1850. To the left of it is a group of offices called St. Peter's Chambers.

Glebe Street, Stoke - 1975
Since its conversion to a one-way street early in 1975, Glebe Street could be described as a race track. The demolition a few years ago of St. Peter's Chambers allows a much better view of the Town Hall. As for the Town Hall itself, only the canopy over the entrance shows any change.

Glebe Street, Stoke - 1905
Hansom cab, Sir? This fine example of late nineteenth century architecture stands in Glebe Street, Stoke, and is called the Glebe Hotel. Notice the brass lamps which were there to illuminate the building at nightfall—what would their value be today?

Glebe Street, Stoke - 1976
This is the result of so-called progress and modernisation—the building has become flat, unartistic and uninteresting. The buildings to the right of the photograph have recently been demolished to make way for new road development.

Hartshill - late 19th century
The rural setting of Hartshill before development took over can be seen in this photograph. No doubt the pony is taking a well-earned rest after the pull up Hartshill Road into the village.

Hartshill - 1976
Much of the old charm has gone, but there is little difficulty in relating the old photograph to the new one. The cottages have been converted into a garage but the old Jolly Potters public house still stands, though the façade has changed slightly.

Hartshill Church - 1905

Hartshill Church was built in Early English style in 1842 at the sole expense of Herbert Minton, son of Thomas Minton the potter, and stands on a hill overlooking the north of the city. The church occupies nearly the same site as the old Hartshill windmill.

Hartshill Church - 1976

The tram shelter seen in the old photograph was not removed until about 1957, and was probably the last to be demolished within the city. Housing development in the early 1930s has replaced the grass verges, but the church itself still stands dominating the crest of the hill, and the trees to the right of the photograph still hold their shape of seventy years ago.

Hartshill Road, Hartshill - c.1920

This photograph was taken from just outside the Noah's Ark public house, looking towards the church, which is just out of view. The electric tram car made an excellent snow shifter on city roads, greatly easing matters in winter for horses and carts.

Hartshill Road, Hartshill - 1976
Hartshill looks quite attractive in this photograph. A new bank and the Medical Institute stand set back from the road on the right; much of the old property has been demolished, leaving spaces between the remaining buildings, which have been modernised inside and resurfaced outside.

London Road, Stoke - 1919

By the turn of the century the town of Stoke had extended along London Road to Boothen. This row of shops was built in 1902. The policeman's uniform has certainly changed since this photograph was taken!

London Road, Stoke - 1976
There has been little change over the years though the old shop windows crammed with goods have given way to the new flatter, less interesting shop fronts. Even the old gas lamp in the photograph opposite seems to have more character than its modern electric equivalent.

London Road, Boothen - 1919
This unique group of houses of Italian design are called The Villas, and were built in 1853 by local pottery manufacturers for their own occupation. This avenue was the most fashionable part of Stoke until the advent of the motor car.

London Road, Boothen - 1976

The trees, which have grown considerably over the years, now hide the houses from view during the summer months. Little evidence that this is a private road remains since the removal of the iron gates, but the small notice on the right is a gentle reminder of the past.

London Road, Boothen - c.1900
The hamlet of Boothen was indeed a rural setting. The canal, built in 1795-6, joined the Trent and Mersey canal at Stoke to the north of Boothen; to the south, it went to the town of Newcastle about two miles away. All Saints School, which may be seen on the left, was built in 1870 with additions in 1901.

London Road, Boothen - 1976
The canal has gone and has been replaced by the Coronation Gardens, so called because they were opened in June 1953. The 1870 part of the school was demolished and rebuilt in about 1956, but here we can see the 1901 building used as a Middle School, surrounded by trees and shrubs and looking quite beautiful.

London Road, West End - 1919
The old steam tram service came to a halt near to where this picture was taken. From this point travellers had to continue their journey on foot. The cobbled path to the right led to the swing bridge which stemmed the Newcastle canal.

London Road, West End - 1975
There has been little change for over a hundred years in this part of Stoke. The pathway on the right of the old photograph has been replaced by All Saints Road, which leads to the hamlet of Boothen and the giant Michelin Tyre factory.

Hanford - c.1900
The road to Trentham from the Potteries and Newcastle went through Hanford. This photograph shows people walking towards Trentham, which was then, and is still, a popular spot for a day out.

Hanford - 1976
Extensive road widening has taken place here, and a dual carriageway has replaced the narrow road to Trentham. Most of the old houses have been demolished, but a few still remain in the centre of the photograph, though they are now partly hidden by trees. Most families going for a day out to Trentham nowadays would go by car, not walk.

Trentham - 1906
The picturesque village of Trentham, two miles south of Stoke, was the ancestral home of the Dukes of Sutherland until just before the First World War. Apart from the horse-drawn carriage, you can also see in the photograph one of the first open-top buses of the Potteries Electric Traction Company.

Trentham - 1976
The beautiful old buildings were demolished in the early 1960s. With modern ideas on preservation, it is doubtful whether such fine houses would be pulled down today. On the right can be seen the entrance to Trentham Gardens, which attract visitors from all over the Midlands.

The Strand, Longton - 1919

Horses and carts fill the main streets of Longton, delivering goods to the market hall which forms the greater part of the large building on the right-hand side of the street. Notice the three brass balls outside the shop in the right foreground—these indicated a pawnshop, of which many were to be found in the Potteries at this time.

The Strand, Longton - 1976
The horses and carts have been replaced by the motor car, but architecturally the scene has changed very little. The Methodist Church was rebuilt in the mid-1930s, however, and the old pawnshop has been replaced by a new shopping precinct just out of view.

High Street, Longton - 1947
The motor car makes its appearance in a city street which had seen little or no change since the middle of the nineteenth century, and shows that the new traffic age is here to stay.

High Street, Longton - 1975

This photograph had to be taken on a Sunday morning; on a weekday it would have been impossible because of the density of traffic. The old railway bridge which carries the Stoke to Uttoxeter line over the main street can still be seen in the distance, but in recent years many of the older shop premises have been demolished to make way for more spacious buildings.

King Street, Fenton - 1919

Barbers Palace Cinema, built in 1910 and standing just to the right of this picture, must be one of the oldest existing picture houses left in the Potteries.

King Street, Fenton - 1976

The changes in this part of Fenton are easily identifiable from this comparison. The old row of buildings on the left has disappeared with the widening of the road, which is now a dual carriageway, and the old tram lines have found their modern-day equivalent in the white road markings. The modernised cinema has now long been called the Plaza.

Victoria Place, Fenton - 1919
Giant bottle ovens dwarf the houses nearby. This factory was known as Barkers Pottery Works and was demolished in the early 1930s. To the left of the picture can be seen one of the few tram shelters erected by the Potteries Electric Traction Company.

Victoria Place, Fenton - 1976
It may be difficult to relate this photograph to the one opposite. Housing has replaced the factories, and the toilets on the left block out the view of the ornamental terraced houses on the corner.

City Road, Fenton - 1919
Fenton, the town Arnold Bennett forgot. Here can be seen the main street of the town with the electric tram car making its way to the next town. The building on the right was erected in 1853 in heavy Italianate style as the Fenton Athenaeum; it later became the offices of the Fenton Board of Health.

City Road, Fenton - 1976
No trams travel this way any longer and the town of Fenton is little more than a few shops situated on a busy bus route. Many shops have recently been demolished to make way for redevelopment. The old Athenaeum is now used as a Bank.

City Road, Fenton - 1920
The tram car on a single track makes its way to the town of Stoke, passing the Rialto Pottery Works on the right. This pottery was built in the early nineteenth century and was noted for its distinctively coloured ware, which won many medals in the Great Exhibition of 1851. By 1934, the works had been demolished.

City Road, Fenton - 1976

All is quiet on a Sunday morning, for it would be impossible to take this picture on a weekday without danger to life. There has not been a great deal of change, but the Rialto Pottery has been replaced by extensive gardens and a workshop for the blind.